For Lloyd & Virginia —

It's a little late for Christmas, but
still meant in a holiday spirit

Bill

Interpreter's House

Interpreter's House

William Dickey

Ohio State University Press

This book is for my wife.

Acknowledgments

For permission to reprint certain of these poems, my thanks are due to the editors of the *Antioch Review*, the *Atlantic Monthly*, *Audience*, the *Carleton Miscellany*, the *Chicago Review*, *Contact*, the *Dubliner*, *Epoch*, *Harper's Magazine*, the *Hudson Review*, the *Kenyon Review*, the *Massachusetts Review*, the *Minnesota Review*, *New World Writing*, the *New Yorker*, the *Northwest Review*, *Poetry*, the *Saturday Review*, the *Sewanee Review*, and the *Yale Review*.

CONTENTS

PART ONE

ANTIQUITY

It is a day of full Antiquity.
The land to a greener surface rearranges
Its rows of vines, the plain white temple changes
Its Doric force to amiability.

Nothing disturbs the lip or the pursed loin.
Speech is a honeyed bubble; it rests light
On the flashing tongue, and any moment might
Translate the imprisoned goddess from the stone.

To move either hand into this sacred air
Is to meet an answering motion of the wind
Beyond which, nothing moves. The sea is kind,
And gathers quiet on the empty shore.

The light's complete.   The lovers, side by side,
Ease to the holy center of the kiss.
The temple finds its sacrifice in this.
The olives leaf. The vines are multiplied.

WAKING

When the first language broke
With its warm pain of speech
Strong on the helpless blood,
You were the single word
My lips desired to reach,
Say, and be understood.

When the first touch awoke
And hand could sense the air
Curving upon its palm,
You the excitement took
To your own bosom, where
It found its proper calm.

And when the eyesight shone
In its first glance, and saw
The various world uprise,
You were the still design
That gave the colors law
To my instructed eyes.

Voice of the earliest song
That brought the realm of sound
Docilely to accord,
Queen of the cymbals' ring
With silver music crowned
And the obedient word,

Whenever out of night
I tremblingly awake
To the world's sudden flame,
You, in your grace of light,
And for compassion's sake,
Tell me my truest name.

WILL

1

It has to find
something unyielding enough
to push against.

A woman or a wall,
anything made terse
with interior refusal

is will's meat, who,
likeably uninvolved
at cocktail parties,

cries, when the gin's done, "I,
monument of granite,
walk on stone feet,

and the earth sinks
sensibly beneath
my power of conclusion."

II

Take only an eye:
a pond, fringed
with elaborate cresses,

rumors of kohl,
billets-doux, soft
acceptances mentioned.

Will turns away, wry
as a bent-necked bird
at the wrong water,

sips alkali instead,
founds its own oasis
where the gaze chafes,

in mica desert, cries,
"I, of the oppositions,
drink to fulfillment."

THINGS KEPT

From the years
when cars were worth looking at,
when they sat the road with dignity and aplomb,
a hint of nautical danger in their construction,
now a parade of ten, a dozen
elegant dragons
moves down the street under its own deliberate power,
with wire wheels spinning, or immensely solid wheels
painted in sulphur yellow,
with collapsible roofs thrown back
like elbows akimbo, resting in thorough ease.

Even in the most empty day
creation can happen, and the ancient cars,
the Pyramids on wheels, the ruins of the Forum mobile,
a sudden fragment of Minoan Greek translated,
shine forth in the pure faith of restoration,
spin merrily forward, with the wholesome noise
of intimate, personal engines.
Red on red,
deep blue picked out with brass,
polished beyond fear of time or road stains,
they lavish in undecided weather
the beauty of making and keeping.

I can remember
sitting, reading a book, in early summer
on a stone terrace, at my right hand a weir,
and looking up to a ring of inquisitive peacocks,
six tame peacocks, trailing their tails in sequence,
tilting to one side their blue anachronous heads;
behind them, over the narrow, ruffled water,
on a small island, a stern stone lion, crowned,
remembering back toward the pulse of royal ages.
Their questions about me satisfied, the peacocks
took heavily to air, long trains depending,
and slowly flew through the pale sun to join him.

Objects, beings that have
the passion and flower of beauty caught about them,
the great design, rising, of peacock feathers,
the sculptured wheel of the maker's admiration,
the bold brass headlamp, the lion, defying night
and the dull years' ability to extinguish,
stand like right faith on their undoubted islands,
or move as gods move, powerful, of clear color,
meaning themselves and the virtue of their being,
bright coachwork tuned, wheels flashing, hackles raised
to hold strongly their inheritance of distinction,
blood relics of an ampler dispensation,
pure peacock blue, brass glory, furious stone.

A LITTLE NIGHT MUSIC

My wife and I purr, evenings,
When the red fire is lit.
The cat is the only spectator
To the enmity we knit.

We, the indigenous felines,
Whiskered and pompous and grey,
Lap up the placid content
Of our malicious day.

"I ate the meat for your dinner
And the sweet cat had the bones."
"I took your furs to the pawnshop
And exchanged them for trifling loans."

"The sweet cat has worms in his belly.
I've left it for you to cope."
"Your three bridge partners are dying,
And the doctors have given up hope."

The red fire is glowing lesser
As we pat each other's cheeks.
She puts out the tall milk bottles,
I take off my boots and breeks.

But the sweet cat is discontented
With himself, with me, with her,
And we hear him the whole of the night-time
Trying to learn to purr.

THE EASY HOUSE

We look for the easy house
By a productive sea,
Seals carrying messages,
An army of birds awake
To our least necessity.

We joke of the subject in
The overdressed hotel.
In the airport limousine
Repair imperfections, hope
The fracture is knitting well.

In transits of cities, word
Reaches us from the shore.
A wave has uttered our name.
The single-voiced rocks have asked
What we are waiting for.

In the cornered nightclub, where
Only impatience lives,
Or out on the bitter street
Where mercury lights lay down
A circus of bright knives,

We think of the easy house
Standing unoccupied
By the sea's margin, still
Waiting for news of ships
On the incoming tide.

FOR AN ASTRONOMER

After the round red corporate sun has sunk
With a glittering smile and smoking a big cigar,
And the chimneys stinking like upright bits of punk
Have lost their brick assurance of what they are,

In the back yard, McConkey, to your work.
The long light shakes, but the longer light is steady,
That has come down the channels of the dark
To find you and your diamond eyepiece ready.

After the searchlights glancing through the black
Die to red worms, their business being finished,
And on the nondescript short order shack
The neon "Eat!" flickers and is diminished,

In the back yard invite the light that follows
Dark stars upon their courses and comes still
Singled from the profusion of its fellows
Like an intention marrying to your will.

After the lights of houses and children even
Grow dim for the long whisper into night,
And the last ship being safely brought to haven,
The lighthouse veils its intermittent sight,

In the back yard, McConkey, where you watch them,
Those stars, those voices that never yet made reply,
Knowing you know the secret way to catch them,
Will fall like willing answers to your eye.

SONG FOR DISHEARTENED LUTE

I

I will praise you merrily
The virgin fair
Of twenty summers, who
Sweetens all my air.

II

I will sing you warily,
With darkened tone,
The maid of thirty autumns
Who lives alone.

For her virtue thickens
As she likes it more,
And she prims her red mouth up
To hide its store.

III

I will sing you blearily,
Drunken and sad,
The maid of forty winters
Who is therefore glad.

For her thin breath whitens
My song with its ice,
Nor her purse will pay me
My music's price.

But she will sing madly
In languages of her own
That she is most beloved
When she is most alone.

NIGHT PIECE

My wife, lost in long snow
and dead of night, struggles to reach
some safe house. Her covers,
carefully made tight
when the sleep began, relapse.

And through the iron arrowheads
of Riley, Uncle Fred,
those men like pointed fences
who disapproved, she works
her body toward escape.

Only the blue-striped pillow
that she holds as a child holds
the hand of a stranger, goes with her,
takes the ice floes in stride, knows
there is some protection against the giant face,

that somewhere the long snow
falling in iron arrows, must stop its fall,
the friendly house be helpfully at hand
where approval lives in a kind magnificence,
easy to see, easy to understand.

EDUCATION IN A UNIVERSE

After the meeting, I would hold you truly
To time, if I believed you could be held.
The flash of your light-mantled arm is surely
A course of which dimensions can be told?

After the meeting-place, I would assume you
As being a body consonant as my own,
But light's king prism mutilates and woos you;
You arc a calamity of confluent tone.

The meeting is like body laid to body.
It is like censing the desirous dead
With the only sacrifice that is unruly;
Cloud sipping cloud, and the horizon tied.

The meeting place. Intact in time and stature
The act shakes more worlds out of gloves and stars.
You are the constant knowledge of your nature,
I swing like planets in a net of fears.

But where worlds touch they touch with a sure solder,
And bodies meet to be intrinsicate.
I do not know dimension. I am younger
Than love, but I will understand him yet.

RESOLVING DOUBTS

SHE   If to demands of others I agree,
Then I will be another, but not me.

HE   If their requiring voices shake your ear,
How will your very spirit help but hear?

SHE   It will, a bird, desert its builded nest,
And in the virgin cloudbank only rest.

HE   If they have wings like other birds of prey,
How will it from those raptors keep away?

SHE   It will seek out the ocean's whitest curl,
And sink within it, and become a pearl.

HE   But when they dive as glittering fishers dive,
Will they not take your luster all alive?

SHE   Venue shall make no difference to disguise,
Nor shall my center open to their eyes.

HE   But if by chance, by force, by God knows how,
You all unguarded should some night allow
Another there beside you in your bed,
Body is body, and cannot lie dead.

SHE   Body is body, but the heart stays true,
And should that happen, I will think him you.

STATIC ELECTRICITY

The celebrations of her night began.
She was as indolent as the fallen silk
Nightdress that spumed upon the still divan.

She was the promise of the lesser flame
Before the candle blossoms and grows quick,
She was the relaxation of the foam

At quiet water, when the tide hangs pent,
Poised for its full swell to the anxious shore.
She was enchaining her own element

Until the music of the night might swim
Upon her wholly like a pool of milk,
Cool, animal. Until she in her dim

Half-motion through the sibilant half-dark
Might cling, as to the hand a strip of silk
Full-charged, might cling, waiting its sudden spark.

SPECTRUM

Brown from the sun's mid-afternoon caress,
And where not brown, white as a bridal dress,
And where not white, pink as an opened plum.

And where not pink, darkly mysterious,
And when observed, openly furious,
And then obscured, while the red blushes come.

SOMEPLACE AWAY

And then she put her hand lightly alongside
The nape of my neck, where the hair needed cutting.
"You are a true light in my wilderness,"
She said, and, "I am grieved at our not meeting
When we were young." I heard the hall door shutting
Where an earlier me had risen and hurried to dress,
Left money, spoken short, and was retreating
Into the well-kept monkery of its pride.

She soothed my hair, saying, but this wants cutting.
My hair was tired, as tired as my narrow body,
Thin with the exercise of staying itself.
I let my lips smile, I let my thin flanks study
The ease of the bed, how the yellow room was ready
Amply and insistently to give itself,
How she smiled in it, her smile as yet unsteady,
And listened for the noise of my heart beating.

Someplace, in an instant fury of knowing itself my body,
That earlier body flicked its brown hand at her,
Reached for the door, and with the door, the world.
My breath rose like an arrogant language coiled
Toward my throat, to say my unmingled nature.
Her hand, a shuttle in a pattern, curled
Through the mixed light and shadow, scribed and sealed
Documents of softness on my answering body.

So I received her hand, and I smiled at her,
More comfortable, my lips fuller than before,
Ready to spend my last cent at being where,
Naked and warm, I could be shut of talking,
Talking, telling my name, the things I was good for,
What I could do, myself, what strong affair
Was measured by the distance of my walking.
These I would tell her, if I wanted, later.

Later.   But now my body lay before
Her body, that confrontation strictly cutting
The edge of sight, till we looked straight ahead
Into that time only of a mirrored waiting
By shorter moments toward our joint begetting.
Then, when we lay more easily on the bed,
Then, when we faced each other, whitely sitting,
Then later, I was not a person anymore.

But part of me said, your hair is in need of cutting.
I stroked myself with her hand alongside
What had been my body, and felt the room approve me,
The world that I wanted decorously applaud,
All smiles, the weather of this latitude.
I felt the sun, the wind, the soft rain love me,
And did not hear, my heart sounded so loud,
Someplace away, the noise the door made shutting.

LOVE AMONG THE MANICHEES

The blond cowl terse as a blunt threat to injure,
The claws instinctive to a triggering nerve,
I am a shut spring in my fanged disguises,
Aping the beast I serve.

I would be for you an offering of clear spirit,
Like water glistening over your spread hands,
Like the pattern described in air when the bird has left it,
Like not yet peopled lands.

Tick-laden fur ruffling for winds of danger,
I gorge on honey in the fallen tree,
Snarl at approachers to these laden acres
That bind their fruit to me.

I would be for you like a length of fallow
From the earliest world, like open mountainside
Too high for the spurred seed to beat and follow,
For the edged wing to glide.

Puzzled, the shared beast lurks under my eyelids,
Dumb, menacing, not able to let go,
Or to conceive that who comes unconstrainéd
Stays the most easily so.

I would be for you as a willing mirror,
Plain crystal, undefined, of itself dumb,
That shapes its voice when you first look into it,
Smiling, "Now you have come."

PART TWO

ON SETTING OUT

The boat is ready in which I must embark.
Farewell then mother and father.   Home, farewell.
There will be letters brought by a talking stork
To say that my adventures are going well.

Farewell then cat and dog and the kitchen chair.
I see you frozen into a photograph
At which, while the Queen of Fairyland smooths my hair,
I may with a contemptuous fondness laugh.

For you are so small you might as well be dolls,
And I am so fiercely burning like a star
That even your petulant ocean meekly lulls,
And will like a taxi hurry me anywhere.

Farewell then old indigenous comfy laps
And nurse and nurture.   I am bound away
To walk the diamond mountain's icy steps
And shake the golden pillars of the day.

Then, when I hold the world like a giant key,
And have no further sky nor sea to burn,
To gratify your natural pride in me,
Briefly, unwillingly, I may return.

DIALOGUE

THE GIANT   Confused grandiloquence.
Like a vast egg
My syllable tumbles down,
Too shapeless, too overt.

JACK   A pitchpipe throat
Narrow as a lady's nose
Constricts my singing
To a single reed.

THE GIANT   Constrained somewhere
In gland or follicle
Lives a slim fop
Elegant as a quizzing glass.

JACK   It is probable I am
Only my self's spore,
Ready in the right manure
For aggrandizement.

THE GIANT My beery hide sweats.
          The spine's ridge of hair
          Erects like a beast's
          In the rude instinct.

JACK   Only canons and fugues,
          Da capo at every close,
          Fiddle my brain bloodless
          With elaboration.

THE GIANT If I could whittle my hand down
          To the gold finger bowl,
          And amuse therein
          One floating rose leaf.

JACK   If on my leathery skin
          Scarlet tattoos shone
          Between the uniform cap,
          Jack boots and jock strap.

AFTER THE ROMANTICS

I'll not go hunting
In that kind of wood,
Where the beasts are all but human,
And the water not good;

For they look at your arrow
With ambiguous eyes,
The sooner to make their sorrow
In your own heart rise,

Rise like the black water
Of their tainted springs,
That deadens the spurt of laughter
With imaginings.

If any ask me follow
To a wood of that kind,
I'll call him bravery's fellow
And stay behind

To shoot my own acre
Where the beasts are thin,
But there's never an eye's flicker
That calls me kin,

To listen to the light patter
Of my sole spring,
That gives only water, plain water,
Not some other thing.

PROTEINS, CARBOHYDRATES, AND OTHERS

Increment, gain, increase—
My belly grows in peace
Fatter than Buddhas or
The heaviest emperor.

Increment of the self:
No Ghibelline or Guelph
Felt his self more intact
Than I, or more perfect.

Gain of the weighty word:
Ponderous and absurd
Analogies from Greece
Fatten my speech apace

And struggle to increase.
I struggle, in my grease,
Half man and half cold fat,
To wear my weightiest hat,

To gain, and hold my gains:
My egg and gravy stains,
Like jewels in my crown
My academic gown,

My hair that duly parts,
My six reptilian hearts,
My simple murderer's hands
On which the live fat stands,

And, by itself, my head,
Sluggish and amply fed,
Which thinks with glee of that
Ever-amassing fat.

Substance and self-respect.
I am of that good sect
Of which the Khan is weighed
In diamonds, then betrayed,

And if I talk to you
Slowly, my voice like glue,
Shaking, my hands like tongues,
Breathing from heavy lungs,

You may know I would have
Your substance to my grave,
And would acquire your weight
To my edifice of hate

That is the only good.
Copper, nor brick, nor wood
Lie on my endless paunch
Like everlasting lunch,

But let them write for me
"He is as he would be,
Weighty," and set it down
In fat, substantial stone.

Increment, gain, increase—
What have we got but these?
What we have got we know.
My belly tells me so.

NOT THIS

What I intended was not this
Grey absence when the heart declines
Like a spent flower upon its stalk,

The bent, the reprimanded head.

What I intended was to say,
Not in all things perfection lies,
Nor are our human reasons pure—

But you set out, as from some shore
Obsidian-sharp, at once to sea,
Where the most drowning waters are.

It was not meant so finally.

Meant as a thesis, not yet proved,
A speculation, hardly said,
The merest whisper of a voice—

But at the sound you bowed your head.
The universal darkness fell
And landscape shattered to a close.
The frozen eyes of hell arose
And glittered where the stars had been.
Calamity undid the moon.

What I intended was not this.

Nor will I think those thoughts again.

FATHER UNKNOWN

The meritor of these verses
Shall be a man entire
Who has indulged in spending
His appetite for fire,

Hot as the blazing center
Of his domestic hearth,
Has scattered himself asunder
To the promiscuous earth,

Seeing the chaste combustion
Man and his wife produce,
Has rendered himself in question
Past any safe excuse,

And shall not have for glory
Sweet home in effigy,
Nor legal kin embroidered
On a meticulous tree,

But sprouts in the wrong garden
Anomalous as flame,
Giving his blood and gender
With his unspoken name.

PRECIOUS STONES

How when the angel
of the golden eyes,
his pupils orient pearl,
his eyebrows jet, and in
half-circles coiled,

comes for his first rich sight
of the broad-spilling world,
how then is he assailed and made absurd,
owned in a minute, traded and transferred,
until transaction clouds his native light.

Reft from the truth
of wealth as God's free gift,
his jewelled heart,
whose lobes are as the diamond's principle,
catches in pain,

and from the precious eyes, made less intense
once having seen the exchange of fraudulence,
the agate tears, the ivory, cheaply fall
into round purses of bland providence
that value nothing until they own it all.

NARCISSUS UNBOUND

Wholly from idiosyncratic reasons, my feet
Seem to me handsome, the arrangement of toes
What an arranger of toes would, at his best, have meant.

And the legs that work up from them; even on moody days
I can see that the deployment of blond hair is right,
And the knee-caps, splendidly defined, not open to argument.

No one should praise his begetting apparatus, and I won't,
Except to say: if a responsible mechanism
Was wanted to keep things going, this is it.

And shoulders and chest; I cannot say enough
To tell how I admire my various body;
Growth of beard, growth of tooth; there is no end of it.

And I could stand by the live mirror forever
Praising my nakedness and distinguished parts,
Save that, at the edge of my eyesight, out the window,

There down on the street you pass, and as I hurry
Into my blithe clothes, the realization gathers
How I want you as audience for my work of art.

MYTHOLOGICAL FIGURES

Whether prodigious as
the cold giant crying
at the earth's nether end,

or designed to amaze,
with snakes fluidly curling
at the cheekbone's edge,

or with goat feet given
to the continuous lust,
the demoniac erection,

all of them like scars
lacing the smooth flesh
of our common body,

or like an eye grown
with long disease shut
to the whole vision,

burn in a blunt light
at the peripheries
of our nervous balance,

beckoning with a stiff claw,
or a hundred mouths, wet
with their expectation.

SHE IN SUMMER

As if she in a broken sunlight lay
Where windy leaves patterned above her head
The shape of summer centered in the day,

As if she lay, and in the grasses stood
Outstretched the summer's kingdom of desire,
Blond map of openness and multitude

Choosing her as she chose the weighted air
To round her in the reach of summer's bed.
Then, when she turned to rest more strongly there,

As if she felt (and feeling, cried aloud,
There in the amorous grasses where she lay),
A king ride naked in her dappled blood.

DE CASIBUS

Only, as in a lavender concealment,
A narrow vein blushes across her skin
Where the fair flesh, withdrawing, has grown thin.
Limits of age constrain her gesturing.

Defined, explicit in her banishment,
She, while the rain falls like a tedium,
Watches the strong young gentlemen posturing
Sulkily to her manifest decorum.

Only, as in a hidden water meadow
A source plays nimbly, transparent, hardly heard,
To the refreshment of an idle bird,
But will not yield to any public tracing,

She, from a countryside half given to shadow,
Observes the full-blooded gentlemen in their pacing
And finds her nurture in comparison.
Amusement flickers in her narrow vein.

IN THE APPROPRIATE MOMENT

In the appropriate moment, like a clock
Striking the local hour's meridian,
She in her hate for hours concluded in,
And never a word to tell where she had been.

Just as my hand, a clockwork, rose to strike,
She launched to the telephone and was not there.
Her voice had crumpled her along the wire;
There was only a voiceless body in her chair.

But when my body wired itself to talk,
And the first syllable engaged my throat,
She was paraded to be marching out.
There was no time for us to talk about.

In the appropriate moment, like a door,
I closed that room.   The clock stood struck and dumb.
She was already someone else's home.
And never a word to tell why she had come.

EXEMPLUM

Quasifantastico, my emperor's fool,
Lay with the moon and lay in tears all night,
His flesh intent with the desire to love,
His will becalmed by her excess of light.

And took his cap and bauble with the dawn
Out of her chamber like a well-whipped cur,
And bit my emperor's servants viciously
Because his bite did him no good with her.

"I would have truth," he cried from that day on,
"Rigid as bars of iron to hedge me in.
Nor lay my handsome body down again
Save with a woman any man can win."

But slut by slut the palace maids declined
And left him writhing on his scanty bed
Crying "The end of women is despair."
And so despairing he at length lay dead.

I sought the moral from my emperor.
He said, "The end of women is despair,
That is a shadow on their pleasantries
And a dark perfume in their shaken hair."

He put on robes of black and a black crown.
With a black band of silk he bound his eyes.
"I will despair and not despair," he said,
"Seeing the truth not separate from the lies.

Seeing not too much good nor too much ill."
The room grew darker. It was night. And soon,
Tapping the edge of his high window sill,
I saw the first white fingers of the moon.

PART THREE

NEWS FROM NOWHERE

The burning ladies lambent in the air,
Like some soft firework blown in disarray,
Stretch, as to touch the curtsies of their hair,
That beckons their bright lips to burn away.

Old gentlemen with nimble coats of fire,
Like snake-tongues dancing on the gilded stone,
Whirl in the measured instant fleet and higher,
To marry burning to the lively bone,

But nod with sleep before the step is done.
Their ladies bend on them a widening grin,
Before the amusement of the skeleton
Bursts, and the red contracting heart caves in.

PICTURE WITH ANCESTORS

Let only a faint light shelter in the room,
And then if ghosts step on this slanting floor
They will be easy ghosts, tacit, demure,
Sure of themselves as you were never sure.
They will tell you personal histories, they will assume
They are the family you have waited for.

Only a circumstance of placid light,
And out of the past, the paralyzed, the dumb,
Glad to forgive you, glad to be at home,
Will touch your mouth and diffidently comb
The shy hair.   What you did was neither right
Nor could it be helped; this is what we become,

Cunning, and not kind.   Who wills the means
Wills murder as the word of every day.
The hates that willed you from the day you were a boy,
Their pinched mouths screaming out the word Destroy,
Spit, and the ignorant gesture contravenes
The old folk with their hands that hold the day.

And how to deal with ghosts?   They are like cries
That rip you in the dead-watch of the night,
Like figured moths meticulously sought,
And killed, and pinned.   Everlastingly on the hot
Mouth of the murderer his murder lies;
Your terrors float like tears upon your eyes.

Only the dead, who know the dead's release,
Can talk to you in confidential words;
Their eyes quiet, implacable as swords,
And their hands tense with passionate accords,
They ask the lamplight, they ask you, for peace.
The manner of their loving is their words.

NOON

Suddenly, in the sunlight's bitter glare
On a marketplace of white, belligerent stone,
The sea so blue it petrifies the air,
Suddenly, in the most securely known
Fixed objects, when the shift of the wind has died
And form is form past ambiguity,
On the deliberate stroke of a real noontide
The scene is less than it was meant to be.

And in the merchant's flat, coined-metal eyes
Some face before the Caesar face appears,
Reflecting past the millenial market-days
Time out of hope of measurement by years,
Reflecting past the navel of the town,
That catches in its cup the ripest sun,
A glade by orderly branches overgrown
Into a greener equilibrium

Of living bird entwined with living tree,
As if a leaf had voice and proper flight,
As if, before the raging sun could be,
They had hovered in unseparated light
Of moons and stars like blood in their twin veins,
Ranges of sky implicit in their word,
Before the worlds like incandescent grains
Were from their common fire of language stirred.

Man under weight of Eden in his blood,
In the broad street, in well-defined noonday,
Sees the green memory of that living wood
Split stone, spill sea, compell his time away—
Then vanish, while the shock of noon still sings,
Leaving him where he stood, there, only there,
Watching his hands, those marketable things,
Flat in the hollow sunlight's bitter glare.

OF PROPORTION

It is the kingdom of proportion,
That being hunchback born I cannot enter.
It is there that the fearless symmetries are danced.

And it is news of propositions
Concerning spheres and other equal bodies,
That they, for their prosperity, act and publish.

But I was marred in the firing, hurt in finish,
The eye judging me neither simple nor whole,
The hand afflicted by the eyesight's tremor,

And though I call music into my partial soul,
The strings slack at the hesitant invitation,
The horns silence on the penultimate note,

And those simple doors of perfect, unclouded crystal
Combine to be closed to my attempts to enter,
Return no echo from those who have gone beyond

The succinct stair, into proportion's kingdom,
There to be honored by the pure equations,
And feel their bodies and straight souls respond.

FOREST

Safe in their careful wood
The maidens ride
Pure unicorns.

No menace from those horns
Nor from the beasts'
Devoted eyes,

White, empty of surprise,
Like water clear
And without taste.

Timorous, blond and chaste,
The maidens see
Nothing but green,

Which, an embroidered screen
Of metaphors,
Hedges them in.

II

Then, in the dappled shade
Red stallions ride
Breaking the grass.

Swollen, the huntsmen pass
With brass horns
And the day's eyes.

Red beyond paraphrase
Intransigently force
Their questionnaire.

The sun's in their blond hair,
And on their lips
The words boom,

As, in some living room,
Nothing is said
But certainty.

III

White as the underside
Of a still leaf,
Actual as blood

But less to be understood,
The unicorns
People the green air.

They are intruders there
Between the sun
And the moon's light.

Discoursing of the night
As if it were
Day spoken,

They, past all language broken,
Humbled beyond disguise,
Subdue their knowing eyes.

CHRISTMAS: ALPES-MARITIMES

For William and Bobbyann Righter

I

M. Port, daily, ritually followed by
A dog whose name I have by now forgotten,
By the cat, Miquette, by three or four gaunt chickens—

If he is the guardian deity of this grove
The olives should be aware age is upon them,
As much past bearing as he is past beginning.

But the green shade plays intricately among them,
And in the afternoon tavern he lifts his glass
Colored like warm blood in the pale Christmas sunshine.

II

We are prepared to own one of these *villes perchées*,
Perhaps as a decoration for the mantelpiece,
Since they are not helpful in warfare anymore.

No warlike look remains.   If the Grimaldis
Ever terrorized this coast they were different Grimaldis,
Having some Hun blood that has quieted since.

As with their formidable castle at Antibes,
Filled now with Picasso paintings and pots inside.
Outside, each battlement is owned by a separate pigeon.

III

It may be the lights characteristically fail at Christmas,
As if to have gone to the market and bought oysters
In an overhanging street, among sixteen kinds of oysters,

And to have bought geese, turkeys, three *pâtés*,
Oeufs en gelée, chestnuts, a chocolate log,
And to have brought them home and looked at them

Under any light more severe than the light of a candle
Would so defeat expectancy, so promise surfeit
As to make it impossible to open the champagne.

IV

Cutting down a cypress is more serious work
Than logging Douglas fir, or laying waste to a forest.
Here every tree appears to have been intentional.

As intentional as the whole very ordered countryside
Receding by deliberate vistas to the sea,
Or the African distance, intentionally obscure.

Saw and axe are not natural growths of this soil,
And though the wood will burn better than other wood,
Still, you have made an alteration in the landscape.

V

Nothing about this picture is that composed.
I am almost a blur, my wife is looking sullen.
Our hostess is toasting the camera; her hair uncoils.

But the air in the picture is evidently different
From that ranged outside this southern Ohio window.
It gives the impression of being lighter air.

The impression is too strong to sit looking at,
As the garlic seemed too strong in the first few dishes.
Sullen or blurred, we must think now of returning.

THREE SPEECHES AFTER THE EVENT

*. . . do not mourn in vain your fortune failing you now,
your works that have failed, the plans of your life
that have turned out to be illusions.*

—Cavafy, "The God Forsakes Antony"

I. A Speech for Cleopatra

As if the blood of the whole country flowed
My veins' bright river, and its map my face,
As if at every turning of the road
I met myself, crowned in the country's grace,
And being rivered by its fertile blood
Grew rich in love, as several channels join
To the full stream, and was its plenitude
Of beauty minted to a single coin.

Was I to be past expectation, then,
I with the river sliding in my blood
Slipping through love as through an arch of men,
Their bodies urgent with their single flood,
Who, single, arched in their full force behind
The tissued curtains of my copious bed,
Then found themselves alone with the night wind,
And I beyond them, on another road?

Letting the river bear me where we knew
There was some moral, I approached the sea—
My mouth a fragment of the kissing dew,
My golden eyes deep Africa's treasury.
And by the final jetty, when I felt
All richness caught in me as in a cup
That brims in the hour before its wealth is spilt,
He rose, a sun, to drink my rivers up.

Who in his arch from the horizon's foot
Stood to the stars, a populated land
Of loving cities paying their gold tribute
To the blond short hair gleaming on his brown hand,
Coursing their love in his prolific veins,
Those cords that held the world in constancy.
Deep in the season of the inland rains
I felt new wealth engendering in me.

And tented in the shadows of his eyes,
While on my willing flesh his fingers played,
In beds that stretched the limits of the skies,
Great in each other, in pure sun arrayed,
Flashing all colors that the world define,
Even past color, to the inner house of light,
To chambers of force where the elements refine,
We pierced, in our profusions of delight.

The river is shallow now, the flood being past,
Keeps only a sleepy flowing in my breast.
And I will sleep, and the great land will sleep,
That in me longs for its deservéd rest.
I was its crown, its golden treasury,
And as I turn to sleep, it lies content
With the magnificence it bought with me.
Wisely, and finally, the coin is spent.

II. A Speech for the Asp

O it was much for a mere noxious snake
Such as I, a thing unnamed in a wicker basket,
Creation of mud, very slime personified,
The shadow under the leafage, it was much

     (I did not presume, and neither did I ask it)

To be to that world-notorious supple breast,
That breast like music from a curved flute shapen,
Applied, asked, demanded to draw the poison out,
The overlong milk, the blood grown desultory,

     (Nothing of offense was given, nothing taken)

To be surgeon to that intolerant malady,
Love, late love, to be cauterist of pride
That had enlarged to the size of a river flood,
That filled the whole breast with its indignant cancer.

     (I bit in cleanly, and the woman died.)

Still it was much.   I left the proper traces.
They would be able to say: an aspic's venom
Decrepited this, that was queen of the entire Nile:
Thus Fortuna: thus disasters to the exceptional.

(Why say she died of being over-human?)

But to have been rocked to the soft susurrus
Of the woman's words, been cradled like a baby
Before it has life independent of its mother,
Been only the instrument of that ripe breast,

(I had not even the feeling of being deadly.)

I had the feeling of being once necessary
In the most intimate sense, like a pleasurable bridegroom,
Like everything fondly male to the most open woman.
It was much, much.   I could have argued against it . . .

(But she had reasons, and I did not presume.)

III. A SPEECH FOR ANTONY

First the astonishment of battle, the pure noise.
After that, the astonishments of love are minimal.
Man, finding himself naked, armored in nothing
But the narrow shield of body, takes to his bed.

Love, I have been your tangle of arms and legs,
And say only this: the bare stone will outlast you.
You bring only the lesser distortions of the person;
The greater, that govern, are the property of death.

I was the man filed to perpetual sharpness
At a naked grave.   Thereafter, the appearances
Of my body, the suave husk flavored with olive,
Had force only in another's imagination,

And from that imagination took their names:
The altruistic snake, the sought-after fever,
The sense of flux that rises from troubled water
And closes in, like thin fog, after nightfall.

Things being so, it is not with astonishment
The sword chooses my navel, but as its place to be
Comfortably at home. That union disinfects
My establishment of the many small cries of women.

For when, in the sensual thrust, a pattern forms,
Its one choice bloody iron, its other choice
The exigent blunt flesh, I am converted
Always to believe in the colder necessity.

It is in the moment when the central fact
Peels back the names that have disguised its name
That the true skull stutters and hesitates into speech.
There are then no flaming suns, no elaborate river,

But the name, Egypt, becomes the name of death.
As one, entering a living room, peels back the gloves
That have altered his hands, made them understandable
In easy terms of reference, I, dying, peel

The skin of love from my experienced hands and eyes,
To become the rigid, the nameless Antony,
The hard stone hidden under the succulent fable.
What if, on the river of Cydnus, a storm spoke?

I answer it now, with no astonishment.

INTERPRETER'S HOUSE

. . . wherefore take good heed to that I have showed thee,
and bear well in thy mind what thou hast seen; lest in
thy Journey, thou meet with some that pretend to lead thee
right, but their way goes down to death.

                    —The Pilgrim's Progress

I

A locust like a thin noise toward the day,
The poise of the moment of morning on its wing,
Tells its slant scale, and in the burnished cry

Says that it will be hot, scalds everything,
The tense heat in the pines, the unmoving shore,
The sand too hot and separate to cling

Or hold the print of who you were before.
This burring speck of voice hot in the grass
Cherishes knowledge of the heretofore,

The knowledge that your vision will not pass
Wholly through prisms to your own defeat,
Or blur to water in the looking-glass.

II

But the shrill masters mesh inside the heat.
Their eyes like acts of mummified desire,
They shout the proclamation of defeat,

That worlds are empty, noisy, and for hire,
House of the senses empty, and the meat
Heavy on bones that hold no thread of fire.

Their voice is noise, the dull continuous beat
Of garbled messages along the wire,
Noise, noise along the nerve, the daily cheat,

Daily contempt their pursing mouths require;
Their subtle fingers move along your fear,
Saying, be one with us, saying, admire.

III

Only in uttermost morning did you hear
The pure vibration of a single voice,
Flute of the solitary, mover sphere,

The narrow tightness of the locust's choice
When he was singing the sole song he can,
His piercing monody of good advice:

That it is bones of fire that make a man.
Inside the apparatus of the flesh
The skull's eye looked toward truth and looked the same

For torture of the body's endless rush
To end all sounds in purely bodily grace,
To take the consummation for the wish.

IV

The masters of illusion wake in ice
To the illusion that they cannot fail
To own again the day's blue precipice,

To clap you in your icy morning jail.
They sew the silver earphone to your ear,
And in your hand erect the silver flail

To move, to kill.   Their memories appear
Taped on the silver screen across your eyes,
Saying, adore me, I am more than dear,

I am your mother, I am your surprise,
I am the lap you wished to nestle in,
The diamond growth that overclouds your eyes.

V

The masters of illusion walk within
Their nettled cassocks to a charm of cold,
Saying, the most of destiny is sin,

Except that sin is old, and we are old.
Old hands hold violent magic, and will live
By blood like bread, in the incessant cold.

What our hands hold they have no need to give.
We give the things that anyone can own,
The wholesale smell, the bought recitative,

The cold-veined fragments of a tearing gown,
A tearing breast, and where our vigilants live,
We are the proper tiger of our town.

VI

White cane correct me, for I cannot strive.
The billboards eat my body and my head.
The makeshift part of me that is alive

Finds carrion smiling in my marriage bed.
The masters taught it bloody on their wheel,
The masters fed it wholly on their bread,

And I am left to feel as the fools feel,
Blind in my sight, in my assumptions dead,
The rusted syntax of a mouth of steel,

A speech that is by sense unfrequented.
Statistics tell me what I feel I feel.
I am a closed statistic of the dead.

VII

Statistics march like stars upon their wheel.
The angry constellations swarm and leer.
Andromeda tells us what we cannot feel,

Draco the music that we cannot hear.
The instruments will not give us safe return,
Show us the star by which we ought to steer,

But stars of priests and tyrants coldly burn,
That have with aging pride declined their heat,
Like the convenient sophistries we learn

In the usual hollow under the pulse beat,
In the hand's reaching, in the hand's return,
In the quiet part of us that smells defeat.

VIII

Only in uttermost morning is the sound
Single, intense, caught in its own delight.
To walk that morning, in the bright surround

Of flowers, birds, in the infinitude of light,
When the grave holy creatures touch the ground,
Knowing they are miraculous and right,

Hand touches hand in that gold trumpet sound,
To say the day star finds its perfect light.
We are the grave strict figures who surround

The masters of denial of the right,
Whose broken hands in their own hands will fail,
Who lose their eyes in this access of sight.

IX

Love breaks the banner of the old entail.
Interpreter, lay tongue to this strict note.
From the defiance of the endmost jail

Lazarus stands; the song defines his throat,
Whose grave-cloths are the precious rot of heaven,
Whose love, that dead love, we described by rote.

But to the dead bones sometimes it is given
To stand in their whole innocence and say
By the skull's eye the imperfect flesh is riven,

It is as it was, gently, on the first day,
When the single word of love came forth from heaven.
And in this world, the word did not go away.

X

The masters of illusion wake at dawn
To take the day they thought was their own thing.
Only the slight-voiced locust on the lawn

Cries, in this contest I am everything.
The first voice, but the voice that will go on,
Alters the sunlight with its burning wing.

PART FOUR

THE LAESTRYGONIANS

Our ship (in this easy metaphor I employ
Calling life a voyage, calling experience cities)
Came next to the country of the Laestrygonians.

They desired us as food.   It was improper
So to be desired, but not unwelcome.
Men sometimes wish to become standing rib roasts.

And at least this desire could be gratified simply,
Being a simple appetite.   I mouthed an apple.
My colleagues coated themselves with mint sauce.

Whatever flesh the Laestrygonians
Most nourished on, we were decided to be.
The intention was to rectify past error,

Faults of the compass, distortions of parallax,
Agreement to disagree, everything that had led
Us increasingly toward a geography of abstraction.

We prepared the feast.   The wise Laestrygonians,
Understanding the virtue of their primitive fury,
Withdrew to sea-caves, refused the invitation.

Uneaten, absorbed by nothing, we sailed on,
Our ship an example of solipsism by day,
Of the space in atomic nuclei, by night.

Stranger, sea-begrimed traveller from an unknown city,
Advise us, you whose arms are only the oars' extension,
You who change plain bread into pure rowing daily,

Into what language should we translate ourselves?
What form of thought will make us a form of flesh
Right to be eaten by the Laestrygonians?

AT BEDTIME

Near the bespoken animals, your face,
Wide, before words, with its unknowing smile,
Asks of me at your bedside, yet a while
Not to reflect.

               With the reflection, grace
Manifests, and the wound demands the side.
Animals stare uncomprehendingly;
We talk together, and are crucified.

Bent by intelligent language in your blood
That from your nature into knowledge burns,
You must reach out to that intolerant good
Strapped on the cross.   It is what language learns.

Your face, at night, sleeping, beyond all harms,
With the endearing animals is entire,
Yet it will wake not to their nursing arms,
But to blind fire.

Talk to me, talk, engage: we are of God's
Most terrible gesture the inheritor,
That speech made flesh that stumbled in our blood,
That red voice of our holy creditor.

Talk to me, talk.   Men in the burst of day,
Their mouths pried open by that ghost's return,
Will speak such words as are intent to flay
The flesh from bone, and mind from body burn.

There is no tongue for animals to speak,
Nor sacrament forces their shallow eye,
But a clear flesh they linger at your feet,
Done and put by.

You, toward the night, young beyond speaking, stay
With these bespoken animals of your heart,
But will fall helpless down the cliff of day
When in your flesh the speaking senses start,

And under pain and under fear of pain
Will loose the animal languor from your tongue,
When what your innocence cannot restrain
Sings your own song.

I to you nothing yet, not law, not voice,
Not prophesier of the wounded side,
A shadow on the lamplight, a bent noise,
A filled place at your ritual bedside,

I will speak for you for another night,
Sponsor and cannibal, your blackened friend,
Oldest of your possessions and most light,
That nightly strokes your hair, to his own end.

But in some morning you will understand
Each goes to each, each lies in his own place.
Then, as the door devours you, turn and send
To the animals the last light of your face.

POST-THERAPY ROOM

Flatness is all. The sunfish lives in it,
And lichens spread in an insistent plane,
Saving their strength. No time dimension.

Flat as a voice over the dictaphone.
Wires, Mama, they do the thing with wires,
As the sea-urchin spits his innards out.

To be the thinnest fillet of Dover sole
On the narrowest china plate, to be dead flat,
Waiting for the steamroller's iron massage.

Mama, with wires. They hang my shadow out,
Opaque as Bible paper, and as thin.
I am a lampshade made of human skin.

They ironed my marrow to a pancaked cell,
And that was me. I was alive and well.
Only the sweetbreads of the past were gone,

The little bumps of glands, concreted bones,
Rib cage and skull, they flattened and were gone.
Oh, I am superficial as the moon,

Flat smirks of eyes.   I gather and come down,
A single sheet of rain, a veil of shower
Falling always in the same limited hour.

Flatness is all.   The book has the one page,
And mirrors have undone the actual lakes.
I am too flat to inflate with lust or rage,

I am too large to be hurt, and spread too thin,
And kept too clean for action to engage,
Or for relationship to enter in.

RENTING

In this wrong house, the objects that I touch
Are another's: that woman in Minsk or in Bucharest,
With whom, on refined blue air-letters, I quarrel.

She is in Europe, but the ice-cubes claim
Still to be hers. I do not own my bed,
Nor anything but my bones and the angry hour.

I will use it for vengeance on her upholstered chairs,
Mock her house cruelly, cry out in a terrible voice . . .
Cry what? "Perhaps we are both in the wrong."

Now the ugly task, to lock up another's door,
Make the alien rooms feel complacent and secure
That will sue for damages if I neglect them,

Then I must write in a thin scream to Algiers,
Or wherever she sits, her ownership like knitting
In a brutal pile on her acquisitive lap.

If I owned my own house, I would be bright as fire
In every room, and stare out of every window,
My face as large as the window could safely frame.

My smell would inhabit the coats in the coat closets,
The stove would burn eagerly at my arrival,
The bed protect me like my armored shell,

And I would be right on every known occasion,
Intelligent to the point of inspiration
I would blind the woodwork with my mastery.

But now I write: *"Chère madame,* it is a pity
We cannot agree, but your objects are against me.
I have been patronized by a table lamp

You will not stop owning, by sneering candlesticks
Made a fool of. A plot, a malignant persecution!"
But I write instead: "Perhaps we are both in the wrong."

WHERE BLIND MEN WALK

Where blind men walk the buildings tell
Their definition to the smell,
The ancient, practised stones exude
An odor of their latitude,
And the familiar living room
Exists by its unique perfume.

Where blind men walk the streets proclaim
That surfaces are not the same,
But burst into articulate spines
Sharp as the Lunar Appenines,
Or murmur to receptive feet
Harmonies of *musique concrète*.

Where blind men walk blank spaces show
Themselves as perilous vertigo.
Green levels of a field of grass
Harbor the infinite crevasse,
Nor effort of horizon bars
The final gulf beyond the stars.

Alert, like radios tuning in
Languages wholly alien,
In simultaneous command
Of this, and an uncharted, land,
Through *a prioris* of our talk,
Eluding them, the blind men walk.

ELEGY BEFORE THE TIME

From Kansas City, the
last bleeding station-stop
of mother's cancer, goes
west and then south, writes
"Having become myself
my fiction's hero, will
pause at tonight's hotel,
called (letterhead translates)
Inn of the Last Resort,
(amused) tomorrow will
taken sudden steps to go
into Mexico, write
nothing to anyone."

Like a cheap dog thereafter
in grey timorousness
will his hallucinations
attend his heel
to lick at the least call?
Heroic, in the bar
back of the best streets,
he, in a diamond vest,
gold pieces in his ears,
muscles like a hoopsnake,
cheerfully will impart
his daddy's wisdom with
new lies in a new night.

Or if that keepsake fails,
the coin in his hand turns
to a useless penny, he
cursed for a male witch,
eyes superstitiously full,
flesh softer than human,
"having become himself
his fiction's hero" may
dance to a smart blaze,
staccato feet bound
fast to the fire's end,
his clumsy hands told
gestures of departure.

Why worry, lovey?   He,
mother in her fat tomb,
auntie on her pension,
Kansas City an act done
in an indecent story,
now suffers his own air,
breathes himself wholly.
And if he takes off
all clothes, smarts
in another country's love, if
he takes off his heart, bleeds
untranslated blood, still
it is his fiction.

But I agree, I
cannot leave it there, and
wait the improbable card
postmarked *Champs Elysées:*
"Everything dandy, death
easily managed. Find
fine company; Ambrose Bierce,
all others who disappeared
stopping by for a drink.
Having become themselves
their fictions, are
spoken with new tongues.
Write to me. Love me. Yours."

NORTHWEST INDIANS

To their abolished fire
Always at middle night,
To where ghost-salmon stream
The abandoned fall,

They, whom my childhood even
Knew to be derelict
Come to the deadened moon's
And the bridled river's call.

Not, in their greatest day,
Those extreme horsemen, stone
Signs of self-confidence,
Statues on horizons,

Nor in their proudest night
Bright celebrants of blood,
Elementals, given over
To the knife's sacrament,

Yet equally with their high
Scarlet-named cousins, with
More rigid civilizations,
They too went under winter,

Found, at the public dam
The salmon at last frozen,
Found how on cold cement
The deer's body unhinges.

Plump, lazy, flexible
Inheritors of totems,
Owners of wild blueberries,
Chiefs over trout streams,

Great exchangers of blankets
On ceremonial occasions,
Nakedness fat but supple
At the fish-spearing,

For a month the country held
The ash of their feast-fire,
Their berry-track for a year.
Now, even my memory holds them

Less and less clear. The moon
Forgets them, in long cold.
The broken fire forgets
Why they should come to it.

Free in the forest, deer
Forget the onetime house,
Walk through it unafraid.
In deepest sea, the fish

Forget the strife at the falls,
The upward lunging, the
Accomplished spear, well-thrown
In the forgetting river.

AUTUMNAL

Shall we, while the night encloses
And extinguishes the roses,
Argue that the color there
Is unconquerably fair,
Fixed past mutability
In the ever-seeing eye?

Shall we, when assertive bone
Predicates the skeleton,
Arguing beneath the skin
That its covering grows thin,
Claim our younger counterpart
From the album of the heart?

Shall we, when the petal lingers
For a moment on our fingers,
But the tree expects the shape
Of a narrower landscape,
Argue that its winter be
Nothing in our memory?

Let the diamond even fail
From its province as a jewel,
Let the sun constrict and die
In a transitory sky,
And the constellations dim
At the Magellanic rim.

Shall we, when the night requires
Our affections and desires,
Argue that our kisses last
Till the blind eclipse is past,
And on passion's self intent
Know no change of element?

Darling, while the roses fade
To impenetrable shade,
Shall we argue they are there
Bright in the original air,
Fixed beyond all power to go
By our having seen them so?

THOSE WHO HAVE BURNED

Those who have burned themselves to the blood's limit,
Have kindled their tree of flesh to its fierce end,
Who appraise the guilty heartbeat, and within it
Find nothing of warmth they can willingly defend . . .

Those whose own hands pick at their sullen bodies
To rid themselves of the increment of time,
To slip from the icy bone its cloud of duties,
Unsheathe it into the milky destructive lime . . .

Those who, in the ripe garden, find no music
But owl-call and the persuasion of the clay,
The cold rock levels sloping silently deeper
Out of the blood heat of the summer day . . .

Commit them to themselves, with the most final
And most generous will your hurt mind can control,
That thought it had property in them. Their denial
Is of any world that wishes them well and whole.

Do them the courtesy of this hard admission.
Restrain comment, think only of what it is worth
To them to be scattered in entire division
Into the blind, unrecognizing earth.

ISLANDS

I imagine, beyond fog, a sea of islands,
Grave with the celebrations of the young
Learning responsible voice, who naked stand,
Shafts of clear being, in the wind's repose.

I imagine, clothed in pattern, a free land
Of equal gifts, where the increasing tree
Affords its nourishment gladly, in ripe wisdom,
And is made sacred by the accepting hand.

How in that place of known formalities,
Those accurate islands sheathed in harmonious sea,
The purposes of occasion daily quicken
To the center of the fruit, to the bright seed.

I imagine, beyond the promiscuous water
That sucks at my step, beyond the driftwood-smeared
State of these tides, a community of islands,
Where the vein's pulse under the hiding skin is bared

And the body stands free of catchments, in its own song
Reserved, answering its attendant parts,
Tree, town and shoal, tuned to their understanding.
I imagine the grace given the silken young

To accept their blood as an interior music
Of laws, as they accept the flowering tree
That wills to live with decorum in those islands
In its own sureness of its relevancy.